Crispy Bites

Literary Leaps by School Students

Crispy Bites
Literary Leaps by School Students

Editor

Sharad Kumar

MOONLIGHT BOOKS

Crispy Bites : Literary Leaps by School Students

FIRST EDITION: 2022

ISBN PB: 978-93-927560-1-6

Published by

MOONLIGHT BOOKS
20 Ekjot Apartment, Pitampura, Delhi-110034, India
Email: moonlightbooks2016@gmail.com
www.moonlightbooks.in

Printed by Replika Press Pvt. Ltd., India

PUBLISHER'S NOTE

Crispy Bites – Literary Leaps by School Students, as the name suggests, is a collection of short stories for children written by the children. Here is a collection of 12 delightful short stories written by our young authors touching upon diverse themes.

Moonlight Books, which has been striving to encourage young and first-time authors since its inception, had invited short stories from children, teenagers, and young adults. There was a heartening response from aspiring authors – school students from across India. Stories of three students from *Delhi Public School*, Electronic City and two from *St. Hilda's School*, Ootacamund have been presented here.

We have selected the best stories from among the stories received and have presented them here for your reading. These are indeed beautiful and insightful stories from our young minds. There is a noteworthy difference in approach between adults writing for children and children themselves writing for children. As you will see, a child can touch the heart of another with his or her creative imagination and child-like directness. The innocence of a child, the shiny eyes of a boy, the smile of a young girl and the grander meaning of hope are all finding a cute expression.

We start our *Crispy Bites* with a daring story, 'The Game of Dares' by Aditri Sahni of The Air Force School. In this story, Kim who along with his equally misguided friend Sam, indulges in a series of dishonorable troublemaking dares until he at last realises the value of the dare his father suggests. The next one, 'New Life' by Sanaubar Fathima talks about the continuity of life as the old makes way for the new. 'Lexi's Creepy First Day of School' by Kavya Satyamurthy is a flight of imagination where a stern Physics teacher becomes a vampire and tries to suck the student's blood. 'The Light of the Crystal Heart' by Yuvika Pasricha is another fantasy where Baldwyn, a young lad and the Lady Commander fight evil forces and rescue Baldwyn's brother. The fifth story 'Together Again' is a sentimental story told by Nannerl Ruth where a badly treated servant maid saves the daughter of her mistress and wins her over. In the next story, 'You are the One', Pratham Bhowmick tells us about a chance incident that turns a habitual latecomer and a timid person into a punctual and courageous person. Going ahead, we read another engaging story, 'The Elixir of Life' by Avani Kulkarni in which a brave and determined girl finds the long-hidden elixir of life and saves her town from peril. Our eighth story, Vanshika Kapoor's 'Guiding Star' is another sentimental story where a girl who cannot come to terms easily with the demise of her 'Google Uncle' recovers from her own deep sorrow and guides another bereaved girl. In 'Librarian's Curse', Pyora Taneja weaves a story on the rumour about a library that eats people and holds infinite knowledge. Srinithi's 'Magic Camera' tells us about a camera that works well and does good when used for the good of others and punishes the possessor when he uses it with an ulterior motive. Our eleventh story is 'The Dream Adventure: I Dream' by Azooka Rawat. In this, two girls who are best friends share identical dreams about Corona, and Covidians who are intent on destroying a planet.

The twelfth and the last story of this book is 'UIP Becomes VIP'. Here we make an exception. This story is written not by a school student, but by a storyteller. Saraswathi is the pen name of Cheerath Ravi, an avid storyteller who passed away sometime back. We have included this story in the end as our homage to our Author of 'Dashavataram' (*Moonlight Books*).

It was a pleasure for us to go through all these tales of innocence, courage, faith, humility, and kindness penned by young minds. Indeed, it has been an unforgettable journey for our children and for us. We together wish all our readers and hope that you will enjoy all our stories.

Ps - We know you'd finish them in a BITE!

We sincerely thank all our story writers, their parents, and the Principals and Teachers who have made this book possible. We wish to make a special mention of Shri. Nilesh D. Nathwani and Vanshika Kapoor for helping us in deciding the title of this book.

We earnestly acknowledge the keen interest taken by Shri R.K. Madhukar, Editor and Consultant of *Moonlight Books* in bringing out this book.

Read and Enjoy 'Crispy Bites – Literary Leaps by School Students'. We wish and hope that as these school students grow into enlightened adults, they will continue with their literary pursuits and emerge to be the future Authors of Moonlight Books.

—Publisher

CONTENTS

1.
THE GAME OF DARES

There was never a morning when Kim would not be confronted by his father at breakfast. Luckily for Kim, his father was not a man of many words; he would make his intentions clear with brief sentences.

This morning too, as Kim stirred his scrambled eggs with his spoon, he was trying to come up with answers in case his father confronted him.

"You know Mrs. Polly too well, yet!" scorned father.

"I didn't do it on purpose," replied Kim shrugging his shoulder. Kim thought it was unnecessary to argue for something that caused no trouble at all.

The evening before, just as Kim and his friend Sam passed the neighbours on their bikes, they discussed how mean Mrs. Polly was to children. If a rider was only to graze against the grass of her garden that touched the sidewalk, she would be out of wits.

"I despise her," said Sam in a disgusted tone.

"Me too," replied Kim, "What harm would it do to anyone to say just a hello!"

"You got it," exclaimed Sam, "How about you going and saying hello to her?"

"Is that a dare?" asked Kim with a worried expression.

"You bet it is," replied Sam with an obvious expression.

Kim and Sam had been playing the dare game for a very long time. They would task each other to flip over garbage cans, pass cheat sheets, break into the teacher's room for a glimpse of their grades beforehand and so on. However hard or dangerous the task be, they never chickened out for they were not chicken. They were courageous and daring!

"I dare you buddy, break into her house from the back door and say hello to her," dared Sam.

The word dare had a very different impact on Kim. For those few minutes, it was as if the clock stopped ticking and so did his mind. Sam was known all over for his notoriety and Kim was the only friend he was left with. The others either ended up with too many detentions and were suspended from school, or their parents themselves pulled them out. As for Sam's parents, they had given up hope long ago. Kim and Sam had known each other only a few months and until now nothing serious happened.

Sam watched as Kim lay his bike along the sidewalk and

took quick, quiet steps towards Mrs. Polly's backyard. The door was locked. Another trick that he picked up from Sam was breaking into houses. They always carried a small pouch of tools that came handy during these dares. Kim took out a hairpin and the next minute, he was in the kitchen.

"Hello Mrs. Polly," shouted Kim and rushed out with the force of a gale.

Mrs. Polly was so shocked that she dropped the bowl of cake mixture all over her.

"A little forethought is expected," said father as he lifted his bag and left for his car. Kim continued to shout in his head, "She is a mean person in any case. What harm could a simple hello do!"

But as always, there was no argument. Kim picked up his bad and walked to school.

The tradition continued. Kim dared Sam to wear his gym shorts on his head and run. Then Sam dared Kim to get Mrs. Patty's table. Mrs. Patty was secretary to the principal. This one earned both of them an hour's detention after school. It was important for Kim to show to his friend that he was fearless and cared for nothing. So, there was no looking back.

One morning, Sam stared at the flag post over the school

building throughout the assembly. It was his turn to give the next dare.

"Hey Kim," he said with his hand on Kim's shoulder. "You up for another dare or wish to rest today?"

"Oh no! Never! I am always ready for a dare, resting is not for the fearless," replied Kim boastfully.

When Kim heard the dare, he was shaken for a minute. Something in his head shouted, "Don't!" But refusing a dare was impossible. He was a trained athlete and climbing the flag post over the school building was not impossible! And as always, he was overpowered by the victory song that began to play in his head when he visualised the accomplished dare.

Climbing the building was not difficult. But it wasn't unnoticed. One teacher, then another, then the principal and the guards. They panicked and watching the crowd, Kim panicked. And then, he slipped. Luckily for him two guards caught him. Kim was panting and choking with fear. He was immediately taken to the nursing station. About half an hour later, his father appeared. They walked to the car together. Kim got in and watched his father take on the steering wheel but instead of driving, he rested his head on it.

Kim was getting anxious. Was his father gathering the energy to shout at him really loud? Kim was prepared for a big yell, that would bring things back to normal. He was really waiting for the silence to end. And then, his father lifted his head, but he started the engine and drove straight home. Not a word enroute.

He parked outside the house and said, "You could have been seriously injured today! Your mother and I love you; we believe you and let you make your own decisions. But, today, you have shown absolute lack of judgement."

"But it was a dare dad," shouted Kim. "You don't refuse a dare!"

"You think that dares prove your courage, do you?" snapped his father.

"Yes, sure they do, how else do you show that you are courageous?" insisted Kim.

"Okay, then," said his father turning to him, "I dare you to do the right thing, always, from now on!"

"Oh, come on!" said Kim as he beat his thigh, "That's just a parent dare."
"And you think you can't handle it, right?" mocked his father.

Kim had never refused a dare in his life, now he couldn't be judged by his father!

Two days later, it was school again. Sam asked Kim,

"Come on man, what's up with the long face? Okay, let me give you a simple dare this time."

Kim looked at his shameless face as Sam did not call once to ask about him over the weekend but decided to keep quiet. He had become too accustomed to the ritual and his head just seemed to follow Sam's lead without much forethought.

"I dare you to sneak into Mrs. Patrick's room and get a copy of the Spanish test," dared Sam.

"But that would be cheating," Kim snapped.

"Oh, come on, I knew the dare on Friday would take your spirits away," teased Sam as he walked away.

Kim remembered his father's dare, and for the first time, he walked toward his class and away from Sam's troublemaking dares. A while later, Kim saw Mrs. Patrick and Sam walk toward the principal's office with a copy of the maths test. Sam had probably stolen the test himself. "That could have been me!" Kim thought to himself. He promised himself that he would now only follow the dare his father gave him.

Aditri Sahni
The Air Force School
Subroto Park, New Delhi

2.
NEW LIFE

As old life fades, new is born. The first thing I remember is looking down from a very great height. I saw others just like me. Here! There! Everywhere!! They told me I was a leaf, born on a tree. When I looked up, the light almost blinded me. My brothers and sisters told me it was the sun and the vast blue stretching above us was the sky.

Wow! Everything looked so beautiful. As I was blissfully enjoying the world, I noticed that every other leaf around me was very busy doing some work. Upon enquiring, my brother next to me said, "There is a lot to be done to keep our mother tree remain healthy. We, 'the leaves' are the kitchen of the tree. The roots and the stem help us by drawing water from the soil and passing it to us. Then the air brings us carbon dioxide that the living beings breathe out, which we then combine with sunlight and produce nourishment for our tree."

Then, I started learning my job slowly. I felt the water going through my veins and the nourishment being supplied through me to the entire tree. I felt very satisfied and started enjoying my job.

Slowly I started observing the ongoing activities on my tree. The tree gave shelter to various birds that made their nests on it. It also gave shade to humans and animals.

One morning, I saw a very beautiful flower blooming on my tree, right next to me. She seemed as amazed as I was on my first day in this world.

I could see that all of us were protective towards her and shared our experiences and our stories with her during our leisure time. After a few days, several other flowers started blooming all around me and I could see little mangoes growing from within them. One fine day, when one of the mangoes was ripe, the little boy that lives in the house next to our tree came skipping into the garden, plucked the ripe fruit, and bit into it. The happy expression on his face was the best reward I could ask for.

As the seasons changed, I observed that the sun came out for fewer hours than it did in summer. So, to keep the tree healthy, we had to do our work quicker.

As autumn drew closer, I learned that all life comes to an end. I saw the older leaves turn a shade of yellow as they slowly stopped taking any nutrition from the tree as the tree itself was getting just enough nutrition to stay alive.

When fall arrived I witnessed the elderly withered leaves

detaching themselves from the tree and falling to the ground. As the soil covered them up, they still helped the tree by becoming manure to the roots. Through this experience, I learned the circle of life.

As the sun started shining again with all its glory, new leaves started to take birth from the stems. I felt my veins stiffening up ready to take life's challenges and prove myself worthy.

Sanaubar Fathima
Baldwin Girls' High School
Richmond Road, Bengaluru

3.
LEXI'S CREEPY FIRST DAY OF SCHOOL

It was a fine day in the Sunnyside city, or was it...? Lexi woke up with a smile on her face. It was the first day of the school! "Woo, it's the first day of school", Lexi yelled. "I think I'm going to be deaf, Lex", said Josh sarcastically. He was Lexi's elder brother, and he was in 12th grade. Lexi was joining a new high school; she was starting 8th grade. As soon as Lexi put her new school uniform, she could hear her mother call out to her, "Lexi, Josh, breakfast is ready". "I'm starving, come on Lexi", said Josh as they ran down the stairs. "Mumm, I think I smell something good", said Lexi. "Blueberry Pancakes", yelled Lexi and Josh together. "Come on, let's sit down and eat", said mom as she slid the chair out from the dining table for Lexi and Josh to sit. "Aren't you a little nervous Lex?", Josh questioned Lexi. "First day of school? Are you crazy? Not at all", said Lexi. "Why would I be nervous?", she said. "Uhhhh, forget about it. God, you are one brave girl", said Josh with a shocked look on his face. After breakfast Lexi and Josh packed their bags and got out of the house gate. Lexi was going to Josh's school now. So both of them walked together. When they reached the school, Lexi ran through the gates with a huge smile on her face. "Hey, good morning, having a nice day?", she asked as she waved her hands at everyone. Josh led her to her classroom and waved goodbye as he got to his class. Lexi's face brightened when she saw all the students in her class. "Time to make some new friends", she said to herself. She looked around the classroom and spotted a girl with blonde hair. "Hey, I am Lexi. I'm new to this school; what's your name?", asked Lexi. The girl smiled at Lexi. "I'm Daisy, nice to meet you, nice hair colour", she said as she looked at Lexi's purple hair. "Oh thanks, just coloured it last month", said Lexi with a smile. Daisy looked at the three girls beside her. "This is Esme", she said pointing to a girl with long brown hair. "This is Lola", she said pointing to a short girl with long black hair and bright green eyes. "And this is Nina", said Daisy pointing to a girl with blonde hair and grey eyes. "Nice to meet you girls", said Lexi as she unpacked her books for the first lesson. Suddenly, the girls heard a loud male voice, "Class is starting, get into your places". All the students of the classroom including Lexi turned to see who it was. It was an old man standing next to the door. "Who's that", asked Lexi. "That? He is our new Physics teacher Mr. William. He joined our school this year", answered Daisy. "He is so old", gasped Lexi. "Yeah, but they say he is a really good teacher," said Esme. "Oh, and yeah, they say he has lung cancer", continued Lola. After this, the girls got to their places. Lexi hardly paid attention to Mr. William's class. He kept putting something sticky into his mouth and he coughed all the time. Lexi exchanged confused and disgusted looks with her new friends. Suddenly someone called out to Lexi, and it was Mr. William! "You there, come here", he called out. Lexi was terrified. Her face turned pale, and her body started to shiver. Slowly Lexi got up from her chair and walked towards Mr. William. When Lexi got next to him, she could smell something really bad, but it smelled familiar...something she had smelled before. It was DOG FOOD! "So that's what he kept eating", Lexi thought to herself. Mr. William just kept staring at Lexi and after a while he said, "Detention for you young lady", with an evil grin. "But I didn't do anything wrong" growled Lexi. "No buts, I said DETENTION", said Mr. William with an angry scowl. Sadly, Lexi went back to place. At the break time Lexi went to meet Josh. She spotted him at the cafeteria with some of his friends. "Josh, over here", Lexi called out. Josh turned around and smiled at Lexi. "Hey, how is the first day of school?", he questioned Lexi. "Not bad. Well, except for detention on the first day of school", answered Lexi with a lone tone. Then her face lightened up, "But I still made some pretty good friends". Josh looks confused. "Wait...what? Why did you get detention?", asked Josh. Lexi explained the whole story to Josh. Josh frowned, "Yeah, I heard about Mr. William too, he is weird", he said. "Okay see ya", waved Lexi as she heard Daisy call out to her. After Lexi heard the bell, she quickly got to the class along with her friends. All of them settled down and got ready for the lesson. "Lexi, Lexi", Daisy called out. Lexi turned around and walked towards Daisy. "What?", she asked Daisy. Daisy looked strange; she moved a little to give Lexi place to sit down. "I did an internet on creatures that eat dog food, you know there was something strange with Mr. William", Lexi looked at Daisy in the eye. "Did you get results?", asked Lexi. Daisy nodded. "Yeah, there is a legend about somebody snatching creatures who eat dog food. I think Mr. William is going to snatch someone's body in the school!!" Daisy screamed. "Whattt, you are really going to believe that Mr. William is a body snatcher?", Lexi asked Daisy as she laughed. Then suddenly Mrs. Lucy entered the class. "Is there a girl named Lexi in the class?", she asked. "Oh, that's me", Lexi answered. "You got detention today right?", asked Mrs. Lucy. "Yes", responded Lexi. "Well then, come on, it's time for detention", commanded Mrs. Lucy. Lexi frowned and walked towards Mrs. Lucy. Mrs. Lucy led Lexi to a tall blue door and said, "In here", as she walked away leaving Lexi in the dark hallway. Lexi gulped as she slowly opened the blue door. The door creaked open revealing a dark room. Lexi switched on the lights, but they did not work. She drew the curtains and frowned. "It's still a little dark", Lexi said to herself. She walked towards a chair and a desk and sat down. She opened her book and started writing. Lexi felt cold and scared, she didn't even know when she would get out of the room. An hour passed; Lexi sighed as she looked at her watch. "How long is it even going to take?", she said to herself. Suddenly Lexi heard a voice, "Oh, it is going to take only a few minutes", said the voice. Before Lexi could turn around, she felt somebody touch her shoulder. Lexi turned around and saw Mr. William's cold eyes staring at her. "Mr. William, what are you doing here?", Lexi questioned him as she shivered. "You'll find out soon", said Mr. William as he caught Lexi's shoulders. "W-what are you doing?", asked Lexi. "Oh, you will know soon", said Mr William. Lexi could feel herself sweating...; then she suddenly remembered Daisy's theory of Mr. William being a body snatcher. Lexi looked at Mr. William. "So, Daisy was right, you are a body snatcher who eats dog food", she blurted out. Suddenly he stopped. "Wait.. what? you really believe that I am a body snatcher?", he asked. Lexi looked confused, "So you're not that one?", she questioned. "Body snatchers don't exist, but creatures like me do", Mr. William said with an evil grin. Lexi's jaw dropped open, "So, does that mean you are not a human", she asked. "Hmm... you'll see", he replied. Then suddenly his eyes turned red and fangs stuck out of his mouth, nerves ran all over his body and he looked terrifying. Lexi jumped out of her skin as she looked at him. "Are you a vampire?", she questioned. "You guessed it right!", said Mr. William laughing wickedly. "Wait, do vampires eat dog food?", Lexi questioned him. "Umm, no", he replied. "Then, what were you eating during Physics class?", she asked him. "I was not eating dog food, that was frozen dog blood", answered Mr. William. "The minute I stepped into the class I could smell your fresh blood; it's been a while since I had fresh human blood, so I decided to have yours", said Mr. William. After hearing this, Lexi's face turned pale and she felt tears trickle down her cheeks. "Please leave me, I don't want to die", Lexi pleaded but Mr. William shook his head. "You have no choice", he said grinning as he brought his fangs closer to Lexi's neck. Lexi screamed as loud as she could. "Help, help" she yelled, but it was too late. Lexi could feel Mr. William sink his fangs into her neck and everything after this went blank. When Lexi opened her eyes, she found herself in the nurse's room with Daisy, Esme, Lola and Josh. Lexi sprung from the cot even though she had a terrible headache and she could feel a stinging pain in her neck. "What happened?", she yelled as she sat down on the cot. "What do you remember?", asked Josh. Lexi explained the whole story about Mr. William being a vampire and wanting to suck her blood. After she finished she asked, "But, how did I end up here?". Daisy smiled and said, "I came to check on you when I heard you scream for help. I quickly ran to the room and saw Mr. William sucking your blood. I called for help and Mrs. Lucy came running. I told her that Mr.

William was trying to kidnap you because I knew she wouldn't believe me if I told that he was a vampire. And now he is expelled", explained Daisy with a smile on her face. "I am so glad you're alright Lex", said Josh as he hugged Lexi. Lexi let out a huge sigh. "I was lucky. I could have died if it weren't for you guys", she said as she smiled at them.

Kavya Satyamurthy
St. Hilda's School
Ootacamund, Ooty

4.
THE LIGHT OF THE CRYSTAL HEART

On that beautiful sunny day in Pistillia on the planet of Xynthian, the flowers had bloomed, and trees were full of leaves and birds. The streets were bustling with people. Kids ran around, playing tag and chasing each other. The shops were full of customers and common folk roamed around merrily. A young lad was sitting on a rock close to the entrance of the village. He was rather excited about the festival season, not only because of all the festivities and joy that it brings along, but mainly because of the March of the Xynthian Army through their town. It was also perhaps, the most important event of the entire season. The Xynthian army was a strong force, among the strongest in the universe. But what made the army unique was the fact that it was headed by a woman commander.

"Commander Moon." It echoed in Baldwyn's head as he waited patiently on that rock. He had heard all about her from his older brother Lobsan, who served under her in the army. Baldwyn couldn't wait to see her. She was one of the most respected persons on the planet.

After about an hour of roaming about, all the people hurried to the gates of the town to witness the march-past. This year, they had the honour to watch it from their own city.

From a distance, all the people could hear the loud trumpets and horns which the army played as they walked on. Many cried tears of joy, but Baldwyn stood there, admiring the gracious movements of the army, especially their commander, Moon. He also spotted his brother in the army and winked and waved at him. He could easily admit that that was the best day of his life.

After some days, when Baldwyn was wandering about the village fields near the lake, he saw something land behind him. It was an army aircraft. But the real surprise was when he saw…Lobsan and Moon coming out of it!

He stood there absolutely still and saluted the great lady when she approached him.

"Greetings Commander." Baldwyn said, saluting Moon.

"Greetings, lad." She said. Her voice was deep.

"Commander, this is my younger brother, Baldwyn. He is a rather free person, unlike me. Always fretting around." Lobson added.

"Thank you, Mr. Knight, but I presume this young lad

can speak for himself, eh?" She said, looking at Baldwyn.

"No, my brother's right. There's nothing I can do except fret around, I'm rather useless." Baldwyn sighed.

"No, none of us is useless, but some of us just haven't found the right thing for themselves to do yet." Moon replied, smiling brightly at Baldwyn. Baldwyn was relaxed to hear those words.

"Well then Baldwyn see you". But Moon could never finish her sentence. Especially not the moment she saw frying monkeys coming at her!

She dove in front to fend one off Baldwyn, who stood there, staring at it in disbelief. Baldwyn was immediately brought back to his senses by the screeching sound of the monkey's shriek. He immediately grabbed a stick lying nearby and assisted the two army personnel in fighting off the monkeys. All by himself, he defeated five monkeys, which impressed the two. However, a bunch of monkeys caught hold of Lobsan and took him over to their ship, triggering some horrified expressions from Baldwyn and Moon. Baldwyn yelled and asked for them to give his brother back to him, while Moon cried Lobsan's name out repeatedly. None of them could succeed, despite lodging various attacks on the monkeys. Soon, the monkeys' ship disappeared completely out of sight, and Baldwyn fell to the ground, crying and yelling.

"They took my brother away from me!' Baldwyn cried.

"Baldwyn, we can get your brother back."

"Are you sure? How are we going to do that?"

"For that, Baldwyn, we need to fight. Are you ready to fight with me"?

Baldwyn nodded in the affirmative, and sat on Moon's back, who took off the ground and went straight towards the dark fortress far behind the town's boundaries, a place he had heard of, but never been to.

Soon after, they landed in a secret base, which belonged to Macros and his bogeys.

"So, Moon- what else do I need to know before I fight him?" Baldwyn asked.

"Just be alert, that is all." Moon said, as she pulled a shining blue flame out of her pocket. Then she held it with her two fingers, very carefully, as Baldwyn glanced at it. Then without any prior warning, she thumped the glowing blue light onto Baldwyn's chest.

"What are you d-," Baldwyn failed to finish his sentence as he saw black and golden crystals coming out of the blue glow. He stood staring looking at himself in surprise as the crystals covered his entire body.

"WOAH! It's the Stellar Guardian Armour! Look at all the studs!" He said, sticking out his fist.

Baldwyn had never been happier. Moon smiled slightly, and then asked Baldwyn to test his armour and weapons.

"Well then, elbow arrows first!" Two arrows charged with electricity launched from his elbows and hit the sack stuck to the wall. Moon clapped.

They tried all their power-ups including wrist guns, laser eyes and levitating boots. However, neither of them could make out what the different buttons on the back of his hands were. Having decided to move on, Moon handed Baldwyn a slate.

"It's a map!" Baldwyn exclaimed.

"Indeed, but it's got some missing pieces." Moon replied.

"It's rather confusing too."

"Calm down punk, we'll find our way through." Said Moon, as she began walking towards the dark entrance of Macros's fortress. Baldwyn closely followed behind.

With Moon in the lead, Baldwyn walked, looking

around, even though there wasn't much to look at. It was mostly dark, with Moon's torch being the only source of light. Just then, Moon yelled, "STOP!" Baldwyn froze in his place. From there behind, he could see two red dots shining in the dark. It was only when something pounced on Moon that Baldwyn realised they were not just two red dots, but they were the irises of a furious beast.

"I will fight it, you run behind!" Moon ordered Baldwyn, who obeyed and ran in the direction opposite to Moon. There he stood, watching the bold commander battle the beast herself. Only when what sounded like the final shriek of beast was heard by him, Baldwyn ran forward and looked at the beast up close. It was a giant white tiger, with his stripes going in every which way, two large red irises, now shut. On his right hindlimb, Moon spotted a red cloth. She carefully untucked it and opened it to reveal a pattern.

"Hey, I think this might as well be one of the missing pieces of the map." Baldwyn said, holding up his map.

"You're right", Moon said, placing the cloth on the slate. It fit in with a bright red glow and there was a whirring sound. Then, the duo decided to move on.

On the way, Baldwyn looked at Moon. Commander Moonwake. The first female army commander in

Xynthian's history. She lost everything to protect Xynthian from several threats bigger than Macros. Never before did Xynthian have such a dedicated and valorous commander. She was a strong character, and Baldwyn was excited to be around her. There was something about her magenta hair, and those beautiful green eyes. It was just then that Baldwyn realised an ancient prophecy about her, "Her power will be revealed when the light will shine." What light? What special power? Baldwyn was almost lost in his thoughts when something began to drop on them.

"Baldwyn- be alert! Something is here!"

Just then, a huge green sticky blob fell between them. Then, Moon and Baldwyn looked up at the roof, only to find…

"SLIME!" Baldwyn exclaimed.

"What is a giant green blob of slime doing in here?" Moon asked.

"Never mind, I'll take this one down!" Baldwyn said, pointing his elbow arrows towards the roof, electrocuting the green blob. It fell down to the floor, bursting, covering both of them in sticky green goo.

Moon and Baldwyn wiped themselves clean, and

Baldwyn saw the green cloth lying before them. He picked it up and placed it on his slate, which emitted a green light which was followed by a whirring sound.

"Where do you think these maps would lead us?" Baldwyn asked.

"Probably to Macros."

After walking a few steps into the dark hallway which seemed to narrow down, Moon and Baldwyn were amazed to find themselves in a large open room, at the heart of which lay a pedestal with a big red button on it. Baldwyn ran towards it and hit the button hard. At first, nothing happened, but as he walked back to Moon, the ceiling started to melt and purple fumes filled the room.

Unable to look around, they heard a hiss.

"Ssssweet Moon, I've been expecting you…" someone called, triggering an immediate response from the two. They turned around, only to find themselves standing face to face with the king himself…MACROS!

"Well, well Moon! I knew you'd come but I never knew you'd come with such a frail human to assist you- I'm afraid I-"

"Who are you calling frail, huh?" Baldwyn interrupted,

knocking the metal cap off Macros's head, stunning him.

"Well done! We have to make sure we knock all those gems of him, Soldier".

"Yes!" Said Baldwyn, arming himself with his assortment of weapons, as they flew into the fumes, aiming at the several jewels on Macros's body. Moon shot the purple jewel on his fist as Baldwyn aimed for the orange one on his back. As moon destroyed the blue one in his eye, Baldwyn attacked the green one on his toenail. Moon used her spear to destroy the yellow one on his head, leaving only one, which hung down his chest. When Moon tried to reach the red one with her extendable arm, the red gem exerted an immense force on her, knocking her at the wall far behind.

"MOON!" Baldwyn cried, looking at his ally who was lying by the wall, in disbelief. Macros grabbed the opportunity and punched him hard, knocking him down. Baldwyn was no longer in the air. His left levitating boot had been damaged, restricting all forms of airborne attacks. Baldwyn couldn't think of any attacks just then, so he used his wrist guns, constantly hitting Macros in his remaining eye, when somehow, he accidentally pressed the various buttons on the back of his hands.

It was then that a miracle took place. Strong laser threads

shot out of Baldwyn's fingers, wrapping themselves around Macros's limbs, making him fall to the ground. Baldwyn aimed at his chest with his laser eyes, focusing on the spot where the red gem was. As Macros growled in pain, the gem on his chest gleamed brighter and brighter, emitting a red light. The gem freed itself from its bonds and flew up above them, shining brightest. Just then the earth beneath them started to rumble. From behind him, Baldwyn heard a voice.

"MAC…ROS"

IT WAS MOON! Moon was up!

Baldwyn could see a red flame in her eyes, and her magenta hair were glowing bright. She was levitating, and aimed at the beast's head, knocking him out and sealing him forever. Macros curled up into a ball, and melted away, leaving ripples behind as he disappeared. Moon got back on the ground and the red flame surrounding her was gone. Both Baldwyn and Moon stood there, staring at the pool of purple in front of them, when the red gem descended and embedded itself on the back of Baldwyn's suit. With its bright red crystal glow, the precious jewel looked just like a heart.

It was indeed, the very heart. The Crystal Heart. And it chose its master.

"Moon, are you alright?" Baldwyn asked.

"Yes, I am, but what is more important than that is the fact that we uncovered the Crystal Heart. It reminds me of that old song-"

"The song! Oh yes - now I remember!" Baldwyn exclaimed.

"The light from the crystal will bring the moon wake, Shadows of red will cover the purple lake."

Baldwyn and Moon stared at each other in disbelief, for they couldn't believe that they'd unravelled the old prophecy.

Baldwyn then saw a blue cloth lying on the pedestal where the red button was. They picked it up. It was the last piece of the map. Once it was scanned by the slate, it lit with a blue glow and a whirring sound was made. Then, a blue dot started beeping on the centre of the map. Baldwyn and Moon decided to go behind it.

There were no monsters on the way to the spot, and they soon found themselves standing in front of a colossal gate. Baldwyn used his button threads to open it, and they found themselves standing in front of a huge glass chamber covered with ice.

"Whatever sits at its centre, we need to find it." Moon ordered.

"But we don't have tools!" Baldwyn exclaimed.

"Maybe we have to dig through it." Moon said, taking out her weapons.

And so, they hammered through the ice, breaking past it, when they finally reached the wall of the chamber. It was sure tiring to dig through all of that, but what lay inside was unexpected and…priceless. It was Lobsan.

"Soldier Lobsan! Are you alright?" Moon asked.

But there was no reply.

"Perhaps he is unconscious. We must break it using external force."

In the hope that their laser power-ups and weapons would damage it, Baldwyn and Moon used all their weapons, which didn't even cause it to crack.

They were helpless. When another miracle took place. The heart on Baldwyn's back began to gleam again, making a soft beeping sound. Suddenly, everything started to feel very warm. They could see all the ice around them melt, and floating on top of all the water, they swam into the glass chamber and rescued Lobsan successfully.

Moon gave her fluffy jacket to Lobsan, who was shivering with cold. Together, the three of them escaped from the fortress, and flew back to the Xynthian Citadel. Lobsan was escorted by them to the medical hub.

Their joint efforts were commended by the ruler of Xynthian, and priceless medals were conferred upon them for their services to the planet.

"And for sealing Macros shut, I appoint you, Commander Moon, as the protector of the Seven Systems. Your services will forever be remembered."

Moon bowed before the ruler.

"As for you, Mr. Knight, you are appointed as the Brave Hero of the Seven Systems."

Baldwyn walked up and bowed before him as well, receiving what he deserved.

"So perhaps, I'm not unimportant anymore." Baldwyn said, looking at Moon.

"No, you never were. Nobody is ever unimportant. We are all unique with our own passions and skills. And you, Baldwyn, are a knight. You are now the Brave Hero of the Seven Systems, and you have the Crystal Heart to guide you. No one could be more important." Moon finished, as they walked far into the distance, outside the gates of the citadel, ready to battle foes old and new, protecting the Seven Systems till the end of their lives. What is better than being a hero?

Yuvika Pasricha
Delhi Public School
Faridabad, Haryana

5.
TOGETHER AGAIN

"I asked for the small spoon. Don't be silly, Daniel can't eat with this!" Mrs. Janet shouted at their servant-girl Stacy. "Sorry ma'am, I was mistaken with the ladle and spoons", Stacy replied with a soft tone. "Mom, we don't need a spoon, there are already forks and knives on the table. And Daniel doesn't eat with a spoon, does he?", Joyce questioned her mother. "Learn your manners, Joyce. Don't talk to me like that." Her mother advised. "But…" Joyce did not want to talk more. She knew her mother was angry then. Stacy worked as a maid in the Brueten's family. Mr. Brueten, their father was out of town for business. Stacy had given Daniel, Joyce's younger brother, a ladle instead of a spoon. Joyce knew it was not Stacy's fault – she hadn't done it intentionally. Joyce was about to take a bite of her sandwich when her mother caught her. "Joyce, what is keeping you in a hurry?" "Nothing mother…I was doing nothing." Joyce said in a weird manner, her words making less sense. She hid her face with her arms so no one could see that she's frowning with hunger. Stacy brought the spoon from the kitchen and handed it to Daniel. "Here it is Daniel, sorry for the delay", she said. Mrs. Janet turned towards her daughter seeming irked. She looked more closely at her. Joyce pretended to be looking outside the window. "Joyce, you look bemused about something, aren't you?" Mrs. Janet questioned her daughter scratching her forehead. Joyce was going to give her answer, but her mother said, "Let's eat now". Daniel took his spoon and took a glimpse over the table. Stacy had made Carrot soup, some sandwiches, and a chocolate pie. Joyce began to chew her food slowly. It was delicious. But Joyce knew her mother wouldn't appreciate Stacy for it. Joyce looked at Stacy, but Stacy wasn't looking at her. Stacy was in serious thoughts. Joyce fully munched her sandwich and the chocolate pie and went upstairs to her room. She took out her pocket diary and pencil and headed to the balcony. Once out there, she looked at the busy town. After a few seconds, she started to write her to-do list. She flipped the pages of her diary and started writing. It was past eleven o'clock in the morning. Daniel was up in his room and Stacy was doing the dishes. Joyce was busy writing until she heard someone say, "Joyce, Joyce Brueten…" She hurried downstairs and found Daniel in his room and walked in. "Danny, did you call me?" "No. Why?", he responded putting down his legs from the chair. "Oh, nothing", Joyce replied with her sentence not completed. Daniel turned back and started to play on the computer. Joyce thought that it was just her imagination.

Suddenly, the telephone started to ring. Stacy hurried towards it, her red shoes tip-tapping. "Hello! This is maid Stacy from the Brueten's house speaking." She said into the house telephone. "Oh! No ma'am" she laughed. Joyce was surprised. Stacy never laughs into the telephone. Joyce kept her ears sharp and keenly heeded to the conversation to figure out who the person was. "No, Madam Finn, Mrs. Janet is not here. She has gone out". Stacy answered. "Ah! It's aunty Finn!" Joyce said to herself excited and forgot to thank Stacy for breakfast. But Stacy wasn't going to give her the telephone. Joyce didn't want to disturb their conversation or spoil Stacy's happiness, so she walked back to her room exhausted. Her mother came a few hours later. She bought both her kids eatables and stationeries. They ate a delicious dinner that day and fell asleep fast.

It was soon morning. Joyce and Daniel woke up hearing their mother shout as always. "Stacy, Stacy can you hear what I'm telling? You're not conscious at all! You're always bemused. What's wrong with you? Don't you understand what I'm telling you! I have been telling you for a million times not to talk to my family members on the telephone. And you did not inform me that Finn called me. Oh, you're a real nuisance", Mrs. Janet continued. "I'm really sorry ma'am. I'm sorry…" Stacy began to cry. "I must talk to John about you. Since he's out for business you're making the house a mess". Mrs. Janet said pulling out a chair and hitting her head with her hand. "I'm sorry ma'am", Stacy said her voice breaking and tears shedding over her white beacon. "Stop crying", Mrs. Janet shouted hitting her head with both her arms violently. "Now, will you please stop staring at me! And to add fuel to the fire, the breakfast isn't ready... God, please have mercy on me!" Mrs. Janet said taking both her hands and put one inside the other like she was praying. Stacy looked at the kitchen and looked back at Mrs. Janet. She seemed pretty confused. Joyce and Daniel hearing everything from upstairs came down slowly. Mrs. Janet pretended as though nothing had happened when she saw the kids had arrived. She smiled and talked to them politely. Stacy put the left-over pasta in the oven. It was ready within a couple of minutes. She took it out of the oven and laid it on the table. Soon the house was silent. Joyce stared at Stacy, but this time Stacy smiled. Joyce smiled back but with a sense of boredom. The kids normally never had pasta in the mornings. Though it was tasty, it wasn't fully heated. Daniel did not want to eat, but he had no other choice.

The children cleared the table and went to their rooms. The house was quiet as their mother was out for a while. It was twelve in the afternoon. Joyce had to come downstairs as there was someone at the door. It was Joyce's close friend Mary. "Oh, what a surprise! You did not tell me you were going to come", Joyce exclaimed with joy. Mary laughed. Mary was a sweet and charming girl. Joyce and Mary were best friends. As school was closed for a few days Mary had come to visit Joyce. Joyce and Mary sat on the couch and started watching the television, simultaneously eating. Mary left within half an hour. It was soon evening. Joyce was ready to go for her piano lesson with her friend and Daniel wanted to cycle. Stacy was still in the kitchen, but Mrs. Janet told her to go and water the plants. Stacy knew Mrs. Janet could do that on her own but she wouldn't. Stacy quietly walked towards the living room as she heard Daniel say, "Mom, I want to cycle along the Parkers' Mount Road today". Stacy quickly replied, "No, that's a dangerous road to cycle. It has…" "Just stop, go finish your work right now. Go!" Mrs. Janet pushed her towards the garden. The children walked away. 'If Daniel goes to Parkers' Mount Road he would be in danger', Stacy said to herself and quietly started to go behind Daniel. Joyce had already left for her Piano class with her friend, so Daniel was on his own. He kept cycling towards the Parkers' Road for almost fifteen minutes. He felt very drowsy and was exhausted. He went down a shortcut as he was very tired. Stacy kept walking behind him. Daniel was about to fall asleep, but he opened his eyes wider to see what's in front of him. He saw a Dalmatian puppy running in his way. He loved Dalmatian puppies. His mother never allowed him to have one, so he thought this was a good chance. His eyes were only on the puppy. Stacy called out "Daniel…Daniel don't go that way…Daniel!". But Daniel couldn't hear her. The road was closed with a rock at the sides, but the open space was enough for his cycle. The puppy jumped down below the rock which led to a huge area full of big rocks and a deep pool down. He cycled behind the puppy as it jumped. He was going to fall down the rocks! He couldn't stop the cycle. He was going to fall down when he was stopped from the back. He turned back as soon as he was up on the ground. He saw that it was Stacy and hugged her tight. He did not know what to say. Stacy took him back home safe. Daniel ran into his mother's arms and told her what had happened. Tears started to roll down from Mrs. Janet's eyes. She went towards Stacy and said "Thank you so much Stacy, I shouted at you for all unintentional mistakes, but you didn't keep that in mind and saved my son. Thanks a lot". Stacy started to cry, "I'm sorry ma'am it was my entire fault. I didn't concentrate on what I was doing". Both of them gave up on each other. Daniel and Joyce were happy to see this. They headed towards the dining room and Stacy bought a chocolate cake for everyone. Everyone ate the delicious chocolate cake. Daniel joked, "Please can I have the ladle back?" Everyone had a good laugh. This was the happiest day in the Brueten's house.

Nannerl Ruth
St. Hilda's School
Ootacamund, Ooty

6.
YOU ARE THE ONE

Clinton knows he is going to be late. He is walking through the streets in a rush. There is a very important meeting he has to attend. He swings the door open and asks, "Am I late?"

One of his office friends snorts and says, "When are you not late?" On hearing this, the whole room bursts into an uproar. The head of the office department walks in and tells Clinton, "Mr. Sebastian is waiting for you." Clinton's face turns pale, as he knows that this won't be good.

He looks at the others, who wore smirks on their faces, before turning to the door.

"Clinton", Mr. Sebastian says in a cunning voice once the door was closed. "You are a good and capable person, but you are not an early riser", he tells him with his voice getting deeper. "The whole world won't wait for you, and neither will I. If this repeats another time, well you know…the door is there." Clinton gulps down his panic and replies in a weak voice, "Ye-yes, Mr. Sebas-Sebastian". "Good", he says with a forced smile.

That day, when Clinton was going back home, he saw a man abusing an innocent person. "Give me your wallet", the man said. "No please, I", said the person but was interrupted by the man. "You want to do this the hard way? That's fine", said the man and kicked him in the ribs.

Clinton looked away. He wanted to do something, but instead he walked away in guilt and shame. "What am I doing?" he kept on asking himself.

Another day. Clinton just woke up. Everything was ordinary. Nothing extraordinary. And yet there was something different in Clinton. He was energetic. He was fresh. And Clinton liked this. He walked to his office, holding his head high. As he opened the door, some of the people gaped at him. It was 8:00 AM. He wasn't late today.

Taking no notice of the others who were gaping at him, he sat down and began to check documents, arranging appointments and helping clients. He felt good to be out of the usual stress. It was as if he had found his calling- whatever that meant. After morning came midday, then afternoon, then evening. The day had been good, and soon it was time to go home. Clinton packed up and started on his way home.

Once again, he saw the same man abusing another

innocent person. And this time Clinton was going to do something. "Hey", shouted Clinton. The man looked at him, his hands balled into fists, ready to fight. He looked at the man, not breaking eye contact. And the man saw something in his eyes. He saw the bad deeds he had done. He realized what he was doing. And that was it. He ran away. The innocent person walked towards Clinton. Turns out, it was a woman. She thanked Clinton and hurried home.

And that was the day Clinton realized that to do something good, you must stand up for it. Not wait for a hero from your imagination or another person. Because everybody expects others to do it, and not themselves.

And from that day forth, Clinton vowed to do what is right, whenever he can.

Pratham Bhowmick
Auro Mirra International School
Sivanchetti Gardens, Bengaluru

7.
THE ELIXIR OF LIFE

Once upon a time, there was a small girl by name Aanya, of the age of 7. She lived in a small house with her parents. She was a kind, helpful and friendly girl. She was loved and adored by everyone in the town. Her town was a small one in the mountains. Though small, it was very beautiful. Even though the people were poor, they were happy and leading a peaceful life.

But one unfortunate day, when her vacation from school was going on, a snow avalanche came rushing down into their town. As the town was there in the mountains, avalanches were a common thing. Though the people were prepared in case of such disasters, this avalanche was a huge one. But no one was badly hurt. Fortunately, Aanya's family was safe and sound too.

Days passed.

Even though there were enough supplies and resources that could run for a few days, the destruction was so huge that it would take weeks to repair. By that time, more than half of the population would have died of hunger and thirst. After some days, when the resources were at the threat of getting finished, people began searching their entire small houses to find any food. Aanya's family also began searching.

Sometime later, Aanya reached the attic of her house. She had not seen her attic many times. But little did she know that something was unusual there. Her attic was not very big. She began rummaging around her attic in the hope of finding food. She went through some old things but found no food. While she was searching, she found an old box. It was small but designed like an antique box. It was locked. She wondered if someone in her family had found it before. But then she remembered what her dad had said, "After your grandparents died, no one opened that box. No one knows what is there in it because it is locked. And the key to it was lost when they died." It exactly looked like how her dad had described to her. Something was inscribed on it:

'PROUDLY BELONGS TO MR. AND MRS. VAGH, 1953.'

Mr. and Mrs. Vagh were supposed to be her parents. But her dad wasn't even married yet at that time, 1953. Then where would Mrs. Vagh come from at that time?

This made the wheels of her brain run faster. Mr. and Mrs. Vagh, who were…… her grandparents!

It made complete sense!

But where would she find the key? She searched around but found nothing but a couple of old things. Old books, utensils, broken chairs and what not! But no key....

She thought about her grandparents' room, which now was her parents' room. After her grandparents died, her mom and dad had occupied it to keep those memories of her dad's parents alive. She missed them so much that her day didn't start if she wouldn't remember them. Aanya wiped a tear from her cheek.

But she couldn't break down and cry now. She had to find out what was there in the box. She had to save the whole village from starving without food and water.

She ran down to her parents' room in hopes to find a clue or maybe the key itself there. But she stopped in her tracks at the door of the room. Her mom too was searching for food in her room, and she didn't like anyone checking her things. Aanya somehow had to get her out. But how?

She had an idea! Her mom hated cats because she had been in a bad situation with them. But cats scared Aanya too! How could she get a cat without having to deal with them?

But she knew that to save the village, she had to fight with her fears. Aanya remembered that her neighbours had a cat. Now she only had to get that cat inside her house. She ran outside. She peeked through one of those windows of the neighbour's house. Unfortunately, her neighbours, Mr. and Ms. Khandelwal were at home. Their cat was sleeping peacefully, sleeping on the carpet near the window. Due to the famine, the cat too was looking painfully thin. She rang the bell and ran back to the window. When Mr. Khandelwal opened the door, with shaking hands Aanya grabbed the cat through the window. Luckily, the cat didn't wake up, and as if that wasn't it, Ms. Khandelwal was also busy in her chores. She didn't notice Aanya carrying the cat. Mr. Khandelwal shut the door with a thud. With trembling hands, Aanya ran to her mom's room. She woke the cat and let it in. Aanya's mom screamed as the cat circled her, angry that someone woke it up. Her mom ran out of the room calling out Aanya's name. Aanya waited until her mom went to call Aanya's dad. She knew that her dad was out on some work, but her mom didn't know that. This gave Aanya a chance to look for the key till her mom returned. She watched as the cat leaped out of a window and ran to her neighbours' house. She checked for the drawers and cupboards hoping to find the key, keeping an eye on the door so that she could hide when her mom returned. When she was checking one of the old drawers, she happened to knock on the bottom of a drawer, she heard a different kind of sound indicating a hollow space beneath it. She used her dad's lever to lift it and it came of very easily. Curiously, she lifted a plank of wood revealing a small compartment. Inside, a small key, the size of her little finger, was wrapped in a soft cotton cloth. It also had a small bottle with a cork on it. She didn't know what it was for, but she tucked it in her pocket. Excitedly, she picked up the small key. Outside, she heard some footsteps. In her excitement, she had forgotten about her mom coming! She took the key, kept the plank over the compartment, cleaned everything up and ran out. "Aanya? What were you doing in the room?" Aanya flinched. She replied, "Um, nothing mom. Just heard you shout so I came to check out on you."

"Oh, someone had let a cat in. But now you need not to worry, it's gone now, I guess."

"Okay, mom. I'll be upstairs."

Before her mom could reply, she ran upstairs. She opened the box.

There was a small scroll in it. She opened the scroll and found a recipe for an elixir. An elixir that could keep the very hungry or thirsty people alive for a few more weeks. A few more weeks would be more than enough for the repairment of the town. But there were no ingredients. She read the ingredients: fenugreek, cinnamon, water, holy basil, and something called Cedronian mint powder.

Beside it, there was a picture with a small bottle with a cork, containing green powder. It looked identical to the one she had found in the drawer. She took the bottle out. Aanya had one ingredient. But what about the others?

She knew that her father grew fenugreek and cinnamon, and she had water at home — very little, yes, but enough for the recipe. But what about holy basil? They had holy basil at her house, but due to lack of water, the basil had been reduced to nothing. She couldn't use that. She thought about the others in her village. The only one who still had it was – her least favourite lady, Ms. Khatri.

Aanya didn't like her a bit. She always looked stern, ready to shout at anyone. But she didn't see any other way out. She went to Ms. Khatri's house. Ms. Khatri was watering her basil plant. She poured a jug full of water into it.

Anger seethed inside Aanya. If Ms. Khatri had water, couldn't she help everyone?

She stormed off to Ms. Khatri. "Ms. Khatri, if you had water, couldn't you help everyone? Are you this selfish?!"

Ms. Khatri turned. She had bags under her eyes and her lips were cut and bleeding. Despite her condition, she smiled.

"Oh, Aanya! Come on in."

"No thanks! I want to know; couldn't you help everyone? Instead of that, you are wasting water on your basil plant!"

Ms. Khatri chuckled. "Aanya, do you know, why this plant is called 'holy' basil? This plant has been given very much importance in our religion. Keeping this plant healthy is like keeping yourself healthy. This is a powerful plant. If I water it daily, it will take care of us. I pray to Goddess Tulsi, to keep us healthy, by watering her. Because of her, yes, we are weak but are healthy enough to live."

Aanya saw the truth in her words. Her perspective towards Ms. Khatri changed. Aanya requested her, "Ms. Khatri, I'm sorry! I shouldn't have talked to you like that. But… can you do me a favour? Can you please give two leaves of your plant to me?"

Ms. Khatri nodded. She plucked two leaves and gave them to Aanya. Aanya thanked her and ran to her house. Now, she had all the ingredients.

She prepared the elixir in no time. Who knew that cooking was that easy?

She gave small amounts of the elixir to everyone in her town. And everyone started to lend their hand to the development of the town. It did take a few weeks and, late but not never, everything was the way it was before. Everyone was happy and mainly, Aanya was happy, because this elixir taught her two important lessons; to fight against her fears and to respect others and not judge them on just one act. Her parents and the whole town were very proud of her. So, in the end, everything was well and good.

The recipe is kept away safely, but no one knows, where it is now. Maybe it's still there somewhere, ready to help the needy……

Avani Shridhar Kulkarni

Delhi Public School

Electronic City, Bangaluru

8.
GUIDING STAR

"Sometimes I feel the walls are closing down on me."

"I fail to understand what makes me repent all the time"

I came back home from school, panting heavily. I was fourteen years old then. Mom tried to scream at the top of her voice, "Vanika, the first thing you do is wash your hands." I was an obedient child but sometimes didn't mind little concessions. I picked up the receiver and dialed to Mr. Google; that is what I used to call him, Mr. Google. He seemed to have an answer to everything; whether it was a mathematical riddle or the directions to my favorite coffee shop, he knew everything. I remember how once my mother and I had lost directions and I was late for my exam when he, despite being in a meeting, guided us our way to the examination centre and way back home.

Mr. Google was my mother's best friend. Growing up, I was unfortunate enough to be deprived of a father's love. However, Mr. Google was like a father figure to me. From getting me admitted to the city's best school to taking me on little ice cream trips, he did everything he could to bring a cheery smile to my face. Not once did he make me feel that I have less of any two parents. He was my guiding star.

"Guess who came first in class, again!", I squeaked.

"I'm not too great at the guessing game, but I suppose it's you"

I got all jittery and nodded a big yes. I believed that the first person to know about my grades should be Mr. Google because last year, when I was close to failing my math exams, he encouraged me to work harder when all I wanted to do was give up.

That day I strong willingly decided that I was going to work even more diligently, for I wanted to make my mother and Mr. Google proud of me, at least in math.

A few days later, when I was attending classes, my mother called me to inform me that Mr. Google had been admitted to a hospital. I could not have imagined the adversity of the situation, but I could sense the anxiety in my mother's voice. By the time I reached home, dinner had already been plated. Being carefree and not realizing the misfortune, I ate recklessly. My mother ate little because she could feel her heart palpitating.

She could not sleep that night, that cursed night. To give

her some moral support and to back her up, I lay down by her side. Looking at her, I could not have thought of closing my eyes, they were wide open and hoping for some positive sign. Little did I know that our life was about to recast completely?

Later that night, my mind wandered off thinking of the day when Mr. Google and I were playing badminton in the park and all of a sudden, he disappeared. I remember feeling deprived of all happiness in those five minutes and instantly took up to whimpering. Just about then, he came out from around the bushes saying, 'Caught you!'. And I immediately felt whole again.

I reluctantly remember sleeping at nine in the morning, when my mother left for the hospital. A little while later, I received a call from my mother, stating the most doomed words from her mouth. She said, "He's no more."

Those words felt like a dagger in my heart. For moments, I could not understand fate. It was extremely strenuous for me to realize and take it in. I could not have done that, even in my wildest nightmares.

I cried myself to sleep, an endless number of times. The sounds of "Why us?" and "What for?" kept ringing in my ears. I had stopped going to school, I missed my exams. Nothing mattered to me more than him. Imagining life without him tore me apart. I became blind to my future and unfair to my mother. Inconsiderate to her feelings, gradually I began to shut everyone out.

I could not resort to live without Mr. Google; I was sure that life would have been no good. My mother suffered more than me, I learned this much while later. Yet, I was unable to do anything for her.

A few weeks later, I managed to go to school, but neither did I speak to anyone, nor did I try to learn. Going to school was more of an escape to me. I was worn out of staring at walls all the time. I had little on my mind, and nothing to do. For a fourteen-year-old, I had been extremely dejected. Everything happening around reminded me of him. The beautiful time we spent together, planning trips, and making fun of each other made me wish for him more. For the longest time, I had forgotten that things were going to get better. Each time I had tears in my eyes, I felt him with me, trying to get me to stop crying. But that feeling was no match for how he made me feel when we were together.

After sobbing some immeasurable times, I grew indignant. I became furious at him for leaving. And so, I promised myself that I wouldn't let out another tear from my eyes. I decided to forget the person who once made me believe in hope and I decided to move on with life the way it was. I hid every little thing he'd given me to avoid trucks with him. I did everything I could to forgive him and forget him.

While having decided to look forward in life, I failed to recall my past. It was arduous for me to think of the past and then to think of him.

I know, life goes on, I know that,
But we would've been better off with you.
I miss the way we used to chat,
Your smile, love, and everything about you.

A few years later, I was called to my school to interact with the students about their future dilemmas. I had been a successful lawyer and wanted to help out the bewildered students. While I was getting dressed up for school, I happened to come across a pencil pouch that Mr. Google had surprised me with on my birthday. I smiled looking at it and packed it in my bag. While on my way to school, I thought of carrying it around more.

When I reached school, I realized how beautifully everything had changed. The classrooms, the ground, the corridors. Everything seemed to be more pleasant than ever.

When I began with the session, I noticed a short, heightened boy, sitting on the last bench and lost somewhere. I tried a couple of times to bring him to focus but only a few moments later I realized that there was something perturbing him. For the rest of the session, I did not speak to him. But, looking at a helpless boy, as dejected as I was, I could not get up and head for home that way. So, I decided to call him and speak to him towards the end of the session.

After talking to other children around him, I deciphered that his name was Aahaan. I called him but he refused to get up. I ruminated how strange it was for him to not listen to his teachers. A few minutes later, I got up and sat beside him. I tried talking to him but all in vain. He indifferently kept on turning away from me. That is when I realized I had to think of some other way to break the ice.

Unknowingly, I began talking about my family. I started off with my mother and he seemed curious. I told him how my mother had single-handedly raised me and how I was deprived of the love of a father; twice. Within no time, he went ahead weeping. He said, "My mother, who loved me immensely had passed away a couple of months back in a road accident."

He need not have said anything more, I got him in every sense. While he was speaking about his mother, I told him about Mr. Google and all he had done for me. Later, I realized that it was time for me to let go of all the pain. This was the first time I spoke about him after his demise.

After talking to Aahaan for about fifteen minutes, I could sense him putting away his grief. I believed that he even smiled a couple of times. Looking at him beam so innocently, I asked myself what more will it take for me to let go. Which got me thinking, that I need not forget all the wonderful things Mr. Google did for me to forget about the things he didn't? I need not break my promises to him, even if he breaks some of them. Those fifteen minutes with Aahaan made me acknowledge so many magnificent memories of the three of us together; Mr. Google, my mother, and me.

As astonishing as it sounds, that was also the day when I felt Mr. Google with me. I could feel his presence and I could feel his warmth. Once again, I got all jittery talking to him.

Later that day I kept on looking at the stars and rethinking how people can see their loved ones through the sky. I felt silly doing so, but I chose the brightest of the stars and made him my Mr. Google. Throughout my life, I was told that Mr. Google keeps an eye on me all the time. And now I could do it too. I kept looking at the star, imagining it to be him and whispered to him, "Now, I see you too and I will love you always."

Mr. Google sang me to bed every day,
My first teacher, he taught me to pray.
Now, when I look back, I try to see,
What could have been, were he with me.

I've begun to think about him all the time,
For he's not with me, Oh! What a crime!
His memories bring me both joy and pain,
After all, why did he end up in a frame?

My tears are real, my agony is too,
What about the map of life he drew?
How much he loved me, only he knew,
Tender and warm-hearted, that was his hue.

Wherever he might be, I wish him well,
While coping with this aching farewell.
He is a part of me, that will never die,
Cherishing him, I will look up to the sky.

Vanshika Kapoor
The Heritage School
Rohini, New Delhi

9.
LIBRARIAN'S CURSE

Rumors. Funny things, aren't they? Some are embarrassing, others mysterious, and then there are the scary ones. It was one of these rumors that led Corra into the ironic mess she was in now.

"Have you heard about the library?" The people she had known said, "I heard it's cursed. Anyone who reads one of the books will be there forever!"

Corra had not believed them at the time. Boy, did she regret it now.

She walked home on a Friday night with her friends, Leah and Alex. Both were dating, so it made her the third wheel, but she didn't mind. Somehow, in their conversation the library was brought up.

"The rumors said that it was located near the forest, that's not too far from here." Alex said, "Wanna check it out?"

"Are you dumb? I have to get back home by sundown, my mom is going to kill me", Corra responded, peering over her shoulder.

"Come on, it'll be fun! You're boring sometimes," Alex chided.

"And yet you still put up with me."

"That we do", Leah chirped up from beside Alex, "Please. We have been doing nothing for the past month and I'm itching for some action!"

"Fine. But if I see anything sketchy, I'm leaving immediately."

The trio took a detour from the path they were on and followed another more to the right. They eventually found the path they were looking for, a rocky clearing leading to the woods.

"Here we go", Corra mumbled to herself.

As she and her friends walked into the woods, the talk of the rumor started again.

"I heard the library eats people and holds infinite knowledge," Leah remarked.

"Where did the rumors start anyway?", Corra wondered. "There's got to be a source, they can't have just started circulating out of nowhere."

"I'm not sure, actually." Alex guessed, "Something about a mysterious trail of books being found by a student?"

"Will we find a trail of books?", Leah thought out loud.

Just as those words left her mouth, she tripped over something. A book.
A trail of books had appeared and was leading into the forest.

A sense of alarm washed over Corra. Something wasn't right here. The hair on the back of her head stood up and a chill went down her spine.

"We need to leave. Now." Without knowing it, a sense of urgency had entered Corra's voice when she called out to her friends.

She tore her eyes away from the trail that had appeared, her eyes now scanning for her friends. They weren't around her at all. They couldn't have just vanished in thin air, could they?

Corra looked back to the trail but instead of finding tattered books lacing the forest floor, she found herself staring at a rather...old building.

It looked odd to say the least. It seemed symmetrical, and that wasn't the only reason.

The right half of the building was old and creepy. The windows were shattered, and the walls were stained. There were splatters of red... paint.

The left half, however, was in pristine condition. Stained glass windows and fresh paint. Not to mention the flowers that perched on the windowsill which looked perfectly healthy.

Corra wasn't having any of it, she spun around on her heel ready to follow the forest trail back to civilization but no matter where she turned, she was met with the same building.

With no other option, she took a deep breath.

Corra moved toward the library, opening its doors. The first step was shaky and the whole room spun. No, it literally spun, the floor was moving beneath her feet. She tripped and took a moment to steady herself.

Corra went into a state of panic. She turned around and tried to open the doors so she could get back out, but once again, failure.

"How do I get out? How do I get out?", she chanted inside her head, looking around frantically.

Surrounding her were thousands of books. Some on

shelves, some lay on the ground and others, somehow unsurprisingly, floating about.

Deciding this library was her best bet, she trudged in deeper, occasionally glancing at the bookshelves.

Her eyes fell on a certain book. Despite the dust gathering on the books surrounding it, it lay there on the shelves in well maintained condition. It didn't look new, rather like someone had been reading it frequently.

Corra traced a finger along the book's spine, contemplating whether she should open it. Giving up, she carefully pulled the book out of its place on the shelf and sat down on the floor.

The cover was nothing special. Its yellow cover had crimson flowers etched around its borders. Though, the odd thing was that it did not carry a title.

Corra, still a little hesitant, opened it to the first page.

"Bibliothecarius advenit" Corra murmured what was written.

Abruptly, a bright light hit her face, blinding her. When she could finally see again, she was sitting at the desk in what looked to be the same library, but all books seemed to be stacked neatly in the shelves, the walls seemed to shine brighter than pearls and the rest of the library maintained pristine condition.

Corra's eyes snapped down to the book she was still holding. The writing inside had changed. "The librarian has arrived", it read. Corra looked around, expecting there to be someone waiting for her, instead she found another note.

"Welcome librarian of the ancient books."

Her eyes widened as her head snapped up. She saw them. Thousands of people with faint, ghost- like bodies. And they were all bowing down to her.

Rio hadn't meant to wander into the library. Oh, who was he kidding, of course he had. Rumor had it that there was a library in the forest that held unlimited knowledge. Who cared if it was cursed, who wouldn't want unlimited knowledge?

He stepped inside and steadied himself. Steering himself to the nearest bookshelf, he trailed his finger along the books as if he could almost feel the knowledge that he would gain. The power, the glory, the-

"Well, looks like we got another one on our hands guys." A voice spoke. Rio looked around for a source, squinting in the dark. He found only three faint silhouettes.

"Leah, would you hand me the regulations please?" The voice called out orders, "Rule 13, never enter the library unless permitted by the librarian. Rule 15, never touch the books unless permitted by the librarian. I don't think I allowed you to touch that."

Rio's eyes widened. "You're the librarian? I swear I wasn't going to open the book; I was just-"

The voice interrupted him, "Librarian Corra at your service. Meet my assistants, Leah and Alex. Thought you should know our names before you became trapped in the library as a lost soul just like the rest."

Rio froze. A lost soul? He didn't want to do anything with that! His eyes darted around trying to find an exit. His eyes glazed over and then abruptly, his vision went black.

Rumors. Funny things, aren't they? Though, not all of them are lies. After all, they were what got Corra to where she was now.

Pyora Taneja
Jayshree Periwal International School
Mahapura, Rajasthan

10.
THE MAGIC CAMERA

Once upon a time lived two sisters in a town called Greenwich. Their names were Sara and Sophie. They loved each other. They had a small bakery which was really popular around their town. One day Sophie was going to buy flour to make some bread for delivery. When she was returning from the shop, there was an old lady whose vegetables had fallen down. Nobody cared to help the lady except Sophie. The old lady said, "Thank You" to her and gave her a camera and said to her, 'My child, this is not a regular camera. It is a magic one. Whatever picture you take it multiplies into a lot of things. But be aware, you should use this only for good otherwise this camera won't give good to you'. Sophie replied, 'Yes ok grandma'. But little did Sophie know that that old lady was a fairy in disguise. Once Sophie got back to the bakery, she showed the camera to her sister Sara and said what the old lady said to her. In reply Sara said, 'Wow, with this camera we can do a lot of good like feed poor and hungry people'. Then Sara took a photo of one of their most-seller cake and it multiplied into a lot of cakes. Then, Sara and Sophie distributed all the cakes to the poor and hungry people in their town. But there was also another baker who was really jealous of them, and greedy. So, he broke into their bakery at the night and he stole the magic camera. And the next morning when Sara and Sophie came into their bakery, they were really worried that their most prized possession was stolen. In the greedy baker's bakery, when he was using the camera, the cakes and breads turned into ashes. He was crying the whole day. But when he realized his mistake, the cakes and breads became nice like how it was at first. Then the next day when the sisters got to know that he stole their camera, they went to his bakery and asked "Where is the camera?" He said, 'Wait, I will bring it'. Then he brought their camera back. The sisters took the camera and said to him, 'Your actions will come back to you'. That very second the old lady appeared, and she transformed into a beautiful fairy. Everyone was shocked to see her in a fairy. The fairy said, 'My dear Sophie, you got good from the camera because you used it for the good of others. On the other hand, you the greedy bakery man, you got bad because you were jealous and greedy for more money. So never use things for bad, only use it for good'. From that day the greedy baker became a good baker.

Srinithi

Delhi Public School

Electronic City, Bangaluru

11.
THE DREAM ADVENTURE: I DREAM

Well today some people say, "Oh, what is this Corona! I am tired of not being able to go out" and the others, "I think Covid is for our own good, we are developing patience, although a lot of screen time is happening….".

So, you all saw different kinds of situations… Some always point out the negatives, and the others try to think positive. But the truth is everyone is fed up with this pandemic! That includes me too…

So, this starts with school, Delhi Public School E-CITY in India-Karnataka-Bangalore. I was with my best friend, Aliya… Oh wait you do not know my name, do you? This is so silly of me; my name is Chinmayee and I am a grade 6 student now (the story I am going to tell you now is about when I was in grade 4). So, let's continue…

Like I was telling you, I was hanging out with my BFF (Best Friend Forever), when suddenly a boy came running in with a pile of daily student edition newspapers.

As I was the monitor, I had to give them out to the other students. So, I took the pile and gave half of it to the other monitor as there are 2 monitors in one class.

I always felt proud of being a monitor, especially when you are the first monitor every term…

After giving it out, I was going back to my seat, and Aliya spoke, "Oh dear, here you are! Read the magazine… Look at the first page!"

I was surprised and annoyed too. What is so important, that it can't wait… But not to offend her, I took a look at what she was saying and burst out laughing! She looked at me and then gaped at her paper, finding what made me laugh.

Not able to locate the reason, she looked at me quite irritated and said, "What is this! I am so concerned about something, and you are laughing!"

Seeing her anger, which was quite rare, I said, "OMG, what is that you are so concerned about… Just an illness that is millions of kilometers away from us! It is in China, hear me out CHINA. I am sure it is just a false fib… Now leave it, let us take a walk in the library later, you surely do look so worried and angry."

She did not look pleased and threw her magazine on the

desk and went to the washroom. I knew that Aliya was not really fond of being made fun of… The next day I apologized to her.

Days went by and the news about that disease kept coming in the newspaper quite often and worried everyone in the class, especially Aliya. Now, I wasn't worried till…

'Corona is now in India too! Covid-19 is very deadly, stay safe…'

The word VERY DEADLY caught my eyes and left me in a worried state. It was Aliya who laughed at my silly worried face this time… I too was annoyed and angry, and my temper is not that good.

That night, I had a weird dream. I saw people were running and some aliens were attacking and shouting some nonsense that I would have tried to hear but it was too faint.

The next day I told Aliya, and she was in awe! "I had THE SAME DREAM!!! That is so strange… Is this a dream too?"

Then, "No it's not a dream, silly, and ya, it is very strange… But for me the voices of those monstrous aliens were very faint."

"Same here."

"This is so cool, let's keep this a secret. I do not want my parents to know in case they think I am sick, and I have to go to the doc."

"LOL!!!" (Laugh out loud)

The rest of the school time was very exciting as we both kept discussing the dream, and not even a single thing was different!

We had the same dream that night, and this continued for ages!

Now, Aliya and I were quite startled... What is the meaning of this, why is this happening???

We finally decided to ask our parents, but we were scared of their reaction and thought we should discuss this one more time.

But destiny had planned something else... We had the same dream, but this time it continued... We were in deep sleep and reached the school late... It was only one time though, but all the people were confused about how late we both were on the same day...

Aliya was now freaking out. So, to comfort her, I thought

we should talk about the dream and try making sense out of this.

We had a long talk-

"What is this?"

"IDK" (I don't know)

"Well, this time I had a longer dream and it was clear… I heard the aliens too. They were calling themselves Covidians."

"Same here, they were speaking about destroying some planet called Azooka and taking over it."

"Yes, I saw myself in a pink and white coloured dress(frock) with turquoise stockings and this time I saw you too, in the same dress."

"Oooooh cool… Well, as not a matter of surprise, the exact thing was with me!"

Rest of the time we decided not to talk about this.

I said while departing for home, "Well all of this is rubbish, and we will make sense out of this soon… But don't you worry about this, and please do not cry like you did in the maths period… Everyone thought you hate algebra."

She said nothing and took her backpack and we both held hands and went to our respective buses. It's a wonder for people how me and Aliya are such good friends. We are so different they say… Different religions, countries and more. But we don't take much notice of this. The thing we took notice of was this stupid dream.

But something mind blowing was going to happen!

As usual we had the dream and now, we were fighting against the aliens.

We had all sorts of weapons.

Then suddenly I woke up with a gasp! I was in a place with the attire I had described and the weapons, and beside me was Aliya! I was so happy that I leapt over her and hugged her with all my might… Just to check this was not a dream, we slapped ourselves, like they show in other movies.

In front of us were aliens, with their ugly grinning faces ready to attack us any moment.

We looked at each other and smiled. Then with all our power we started a war with the aliens. IDK (I don't know), if you know the GENSHIN IMPACT game, well if you do, you might know all the powers, weapons, and stuff they have… Both of us had the same thing!

We enjoyed it very much and forgot about school stuff, all the discussion… And of course, like all the movies or stories have good endings (well they do, mostly) we did too. We won against the aliens, but in the end I kind of, I repeat, I KIND OF cried. This was all so fun and who would not want to live this kind of life forever and be with their BFF's forever. Aliya comforted me and we both were transported back to where we came from, our beds of course!

Then we slept and we had a dream, again but this time, we were not worried because we had had our adventure. In the dream we saw a magical creature, speaking to us, comforting us, and thanking us for protecting their kingdom from the COVIDIANS.

We did think that they were lucky they got rid of the COVIDIANS… We wished we did too, from this COVID-19!

In school, we both met and smiled as we knew what had happened…

We did not talk about it though… If we did, one of us would surely start to cry or sob because the adventure ended…

Nothing this extraordinary happened to us anymore that term and I really did wish it would… Now we all are locked up in our houses… But that cannot stop us from having an adventure, can it? So, yes you all guessed it, I did have many adventures with many people… But that is for some other time. For now, we all can wait and see what happens next!

Azooka Chinmayee Rawat
Delhi Public School
Electronic City, Bangalore

12.
UIP BECOMES VIP

"Master, Poverty Amma wants to see you", a boy said.

"Who is that Poverty Amma?", the Master asked.

"That stingy devil of a Bhadrakali of this house", the boy replied.

The boy is the servant of that household. He has only contempt and hatred towards his employer. Unnecessarily she will quarrel with the servants and will not pay their wages properly. Parootty Amma's original name was Parukutty. When she became popular in the locality as a money bag, she changed her name to Parootty thinking that the original name given by her parents was very outdated.

The servant boy knows a little English. He has studied up to 8th standard. Even though he was good in his studies, he could not continue his education. He got employed in this house. Though he was afraid to call the mistress 'Poverty Amma' to her face, to outsiders he would always address her disparagingly as 'that stingy devil, Poverty Amma' since she has always been mean and cruel towards him.

The Master slowly entered the compound and stood respectfully in the courtyard. Parootty Amma was sitting on an easy chair with both legs stretched out in front of her. When her daughter Kamala saw the Master, she came out running. It was on account of Kamala's obstinate request that Parootty sent for the Master. She had asked her mother to give a wedding invitation to the Master. Parootty became angry as she considered it all below her status to invite such low people for her daughter's marriage. As a last resort, to dissuade Kamala, she asked, "Is it essential to invite this low type of Master? Other invitees are all money bags, cinema stars, politicians, and very senior government officers."

Kamala liked and respected the Master. He was a very good man who loved his students and respected all people. Kamala insisted and said, "I want my Master to attend my wedding. Even if all the other money bags, cinema stars, officers and politicians do not come for the wedding, I won't care in the least. But my Master should come."

Since she could not hurt her only daughter, Parootty took an invitation in her left hand and threw it on the floor and said, "Give it to your Guru Bhootan" to express her anger and contempt. Kamala took it and went to the Master and with great respect, gave it to her dear Master and touched his feet. The Master blessed her saying, "Sowbhagyavathi Bhava" (Be a happily married woman) and went away.

The Master thought: "How can I participate in the wedding in such a rich family? Usually, people in general have only contempt for Masters. Not only that, I am a poor typing Master now; I remember on many occasions how I have been neglected in the company of big people."

"Many times, I have been referred to with contempt. Even my relatives speak about me with contempt. But when they need any type of help, they will approach only this Balan (that is the Master's name). One day, when my younger brothers, nephews and other friends were assembled in a relative's house, a distinguished guest happened to come there. I was the oldest among them. The host introduced all those who were there except me like this: -

This is my sister's husband, Raman Menon, Deputy General Manager in LIC; this man is my wife's brother, Damodaran, Personnel Manager in Southern Railways; this is Gopalakrishnan Nair, a good friend of mine, Customs Superintendent. Like this, all except me were introduced. Then that gentleman pointing at me asked "Who is this old gentleman?"

The host replied: Oh! He is a resident of this locality - a Master.

Then one youngster interrupted and said, "a Master who teaches typing to the slum children." The Master recollected those events.

"Taking this as a joke, all except that distinguished guest laughed. This so-called youngster had taken my help to draft, type and even post his application for a job in an insurance company as he had no earnings then. Even when he was selected for the job, since he had no money for his travel to his work spot, it was I who gave him money. That is, even though he had a rich uncle living quite near his house, another uncle who was a lakhpati or a millionaire who lived in the nearest town, and brothers-in-law who held high positions in the government service. But it was only the slum children's Master who readily came to his help." Thinking along these lines, the Master made his way homeward.

Now we will move on to the details of Parootty and her sister Madhootty. When her elder sister adopted the new name Parootty, Madhavi Kutty changed her name to MadhuKutty. Parootty out of great affection would call her younger sister, Madhootty. When the servants talked among themselves and occasionally to select outsiders, they will say Poverty Amma and Madhu Kuthi Amma. If they are asked, "Why do you say Kuthi?", then their answer, "In Hindi, Kuthi means 'dog', so, Kuthi means 'bitch.'"

It is due to the opulence of her elder sister that Madhootty could also pretend to be rich. Parootty married twice. Kamala was born of the first husband. Kamala is a really beautiful girl and is very humble. She has no arrogance usually found in the children of rich parents. Her father died when she was a child, and her mother married a very rich Tamil Chettiar. This Chettiar was not content with one wife. So Madhootty also became his wife. This did not create any ill-feeling between the sisters. On the other hand, it strengthened their affection for each other. The Chettiar had one or two textile mills and he owned a private bank. With the utmost cunningness, the sisters got the ownership of these establishments transferred into Parootty's name and gradually he was kicked out of their life. Now apart from the income from the mills and the bank, they have the dubious sources of income. By joining hands with smugglers and counterfeit currency printing gangs, they acquired a lot and became very rich. Kamala is the only heir to all this fortune.

The wedding day arrived. The wedding was to take place in a very expensive marriage hall. All the arrangements were of top variety. CCTVs were fixed in appropriate places. The whole hall was illuminated and decorated. All sorts of rich food items were kept in the dining area. A board "Only For VIPs" was kept in the first row of chairs. That was meant for VIPs and their henchmen only. Only the big money bags, top ranking cinema stars and politicians were meant to occupy those chairs. If anybody else by mistake occupied any of those chairs, Parootty's volunteers would politely ask them to vacate their seat and sit in some other row.

The Muhurtham (auspicious hour) was fixed between 7 p.m. and 8:30 p.m. The local MP, Mr. Padmanabhan Nair was the Chief Guest, and it was decided that he should give the wedding garland to the couple. The invitees started coming one by one and in groups. The VIPs were ushered to their seats in the first row by the volunteers. Others had to find their own seats anywhere else in the hall. The invitees were welcomed at the entrance by Parootty and Madhootty depending on their status by folded hands, handshake, and embrace. The ordinary invitees had to be satisfied with a smile. Only money bags and cinema stars with no exception received the most affectionate embrace from both the sisters. By this time, the whole hall was filled and except some chairs in the reserved first row, all other seats were occupied.

Then the Master arrived with his old walking stick. He was not received even with a smile by anybody. When he found that there was no vacant chair in all the rows he sat on a vacant chair in the front row. He had not seen the reservation board kept there. Seeing the Master seated there, the Volunteer Captain came and told the Master that that row was reserved for VIPs and he should move out and occupy a chair somewhere else. The Master slowly got up and went searching for a vacant chair somewhere else. But he could not find a chair to sit. Even when so many youngsters sitting on chairs saw the Master unsuccessfully searching for a seat, nobody thought of offering him a seat. Finally, he walked to the extreme end of the hall where the servants were standing and stood with them.

The clock struck eight. Even then the Chief Guest had not arrived. All were anxiously waiting for his arrival. Parootty and Madhootty were keeping their eyes fixed on the road suppressing their anxiety behind artificial smiles. Volunteers were frequently going to the road and returning with disappointment. Then all of a sudden, the sound of a car horn was heard in succession. The volunteers, Parootty, and Madhootty ran to the road. The car carrying the MP came and stood in front of the gate with a screech. The driver came out and opened the door and Padmanabhan Nair came out with folded hands. A smiling Parootty took the flower garland from the Volunteer Captain and garlanded the MP. Madhootty presented him with a bouquet.

Escorted by Parootty and Madhootty on both sides and followed by various party workers and volunteers, the MP came and occupied the specially arranged seat of the Chief Guest. Parootty and Madhootty sat on either side flanking him. Then ensued a scramble for chairs in the VIP row as you witness in a game of children's musical chairs. One politician trying to get a chair in hurry sat on the lap of a lady by mistake. She pushed him out, to the delight of the onlookers. In another case, the volunteer had to intercede to separate two people who sat together on the same chair. Those who failed to get a seat had to move away with a disappointed smile and stand on the side.

After exchanging some pleasantries with the MP, Parootty climbed on the stage, gave a small speech in English sprinkled with Malayalam words. Then she requested the MP to hand over the wedding garlands to the bride and groom and to bless them. With a smiling face, the MP climbed upon the stage with folded hands. Then in the way the politicians do, he looked at the audience from one end of the hall to the other. Suddenly he got excited. Was that not his most dear Master who was standing with a walking stick, leaning on it for support, in the company of the servants? In one moment Padmanabhan Nair recollected his childhood, when he was a small kid and also a student in the fourth form. The person standing at the back of the hall was none other than his dear 'Balettan', who later became his 'Balan Master'.

When he was studying in Elementary school, Balettan used to buy him chocolates, used to tell him stories of ghosts and animals, and tease him with humorous jokes. One day when he fell into the pond and was struggling to float, Balettan jumped fully clothed into the pond and rescued him. After Balettan completed his college education, he joined the same school as a teacher. Luckily, Balettan became his class teacher in the ninth standard. Balan Master was treated with the utmost respect and love by all the 45 students of the class. Even the students who would tell lies to other teachers would not tell a lie to Balan Master. Before the completion of that academic year, the Master resigned his job as he secured a better position in a far-off country. Even when the Master told them not to arrange a send-off party, the students arranged one. The Head Master presided over the function even though he personally did not like Balan Master. The students presented a 'Mangalapatram' (a vessel filled with holy water) to their master and the student leader garlanded him. Many students spoke good words about their master. As a mere formality, the Head Master also spoke a few words. By the time the function was over, all the ninety eyes were brimming with tears. Some students even burst out crying loudly. To the Head Master, this came as a shock. He had never understood that this teacher whom he had ill-treated several times was the darling of the students. Thus, the Master also took leave of his dear students with folded hands and tears in his eyes.

Now after thirty years, the MP was seeing his dear Guru. His heart throbbed with delight, and he wanted to rush over to his dear Master. However, remembering that he was the Chief Guest and that the guests were waiting for him to speak, he said: "I am glad that Parootty Amma has invited me to perform the task of giving the wedding garlands to the bride and the groom. But there is a VVIP in this hall who is more suitable than me to do that. I will bring that great man to the stage".

Saying this, he climbed down from the stage and started walking towards the end of the hall. Parootty, Madhootty and the Volunteer Captain followed the MP. Each and every money bag and cinema star thought that the MP had him/her in mind when he made this announcement. So, they all got mentally prepared to come to the stage as the VVIP. But, disappointing all of them, the MP walked to the tail end of the hall where the servants were standing.

Then he came before his Guru and asked: "Do you recognise me, Sir? I am Pappan whom you taught in the ninth standard". He bowed and touched his Master's feet. It is difficult to say who was more happy - the Master or the student. They embraced each other.

The MP took hold of his Master's hand and led him onto the stage. When Madhootty, Parootty and the Volunteer Captain who had asked the Master to vacate the chair were looking on with wonder, the MP took the wedding garlands and handed over the same to the Master requesting him to give the garlands to the bride and groom and bless them.

Keeping his walking stick on a nearby chair, the Master gave a garland first to the bride and when she had garlanded the groom, he gave the next one to the groom. The groom then garlanded the bride. Then the couple touched the feet of the Master and the pious old man blessed them both, "Have a happy married life."

The poor Institute Master now got the real reward for all.

His long years of work and service to the students had seen its rewards. It was the real love and devotion shining as unshed tears in his former student's eyes. MP Padmanabhan Nair looked on happily as he had fulfilled his greatest desire to honour his dearest Balan Master as a Very Very Important Person. A UIP (Unimportant Person) had become a VIP (Very Important Person).

Saraswathi

RELATED BOOKS

Title : HONEYBEE MOONLIGHT STORIES–SET 1
Author : R K Madhukar
ISBN PB : 978-93-9275-667-2
Price : Rs.1250/-
Set 1 : A Pack of 10 Books
Pages : 160 (each book 16 pages)
Size : 8.5" x 11"/22 cm x 28 cm
Year of Publication: 2022
Rights : World Rights

About the Series

Honeybees are known for their skill of collecting nectar from a variety of flowers and transforming it into delicious honey. "Honeybee" here refers to the author's name. "Madhukar" in Sanskrit means honeybee. These exclusive stories brought to you from distant lands and different cultures carry the irresistible charm of ancient storytelling, orally passed on from generation to generation, by peoples across the world. Moonlight Books brings to you these delightful folktales and stories with captivating pictures and enchanting colors, like the soothing allure of the moonlight. The Honeybee Moonlight series covers 20 books, and the first set of 10 books is presented here. A humble effort at enriching children's literature, these stories are written in a simple, lucid, and endearing style. Adorable Stories that children would enjoy reading Again and Again.

1. Mostafa And The Sea Queen (Egypt)
2. Prince Faisal And His Magnificent Sword (Iraq)
3. The Beggar King's Gracious Daughter (China)
4. The Grateful Animals And The Ungrateful Man (India)
5. The Mermaid Who Comes To Earth (Scotland)
6. The Priceless Shabby Gift (Israel)
7. The Mischievous Monkey Goes For A Shave (Brazil)
8. The Three Identical Dolls (India\Mongolia)
9. The Ugly Bird Curses The Princess (Kenya)
10. Theseus and Minotaur (Greece)

About the Author

R. K. Madhukar, a prolific writer, is a Retired Banker based in Bangalore. He has written books on a variety of subjects for over 30 years. His books cover several genres including Bank Marketing, Business Communication, Managerial Skill Development, and the Spiritual Wisdom of India. His books on Business Communication are widely prescribed by Universities and Institutes across India for their Commerce, Management, and other Professional Courses. Shri Madhukar is at present the Editor and Consultant of Moonlight Books, Delhi. He is now focusing on writing Children's Books. His two recent books, 'Enchanting Stories from India and Abroad' & 'Fabulous Folktales from India and Abroad' have received a heartening response in India and USA.

Title : Fabulous Folktales from India and Abroad
Author : R.K.Madhukar
Pages : 264
Edition : Paperback¬
Price : Rs.350/-
ISBN : 978-81-9445-08-5-6
EISBN : 978-81-9445-08-6-3
Year of Publication: 2020
Worldrights

About the Book:

Folktales, as we know, are stories passed on from generation to generation orally. Folktales of enormous variety have endeared people across countries since time immemorial. These folktales take the readers back to a world that existed hundreds and even thousands of years ago.

This book brings to you another fabulous collection of 12 meticulously selected, intensely researched folktales from 10 different countries. Folktales presented here come to us from Iraq, Israel, Turkey, Middle East, Germany, Czechoslovakia, Denmark, Germany, Scotland and Hawaii (USA), besides India.

These are very absorbing and engaging stories; stories children and adults would love to read. As the children and adults read these stories, they get a feel of geography, history and a sense of ancient culture. Further, an insight into the idioms and phrases, word pairs and exposure to strong and vibrant words inbuilt into this book aids young readers in making their conversation better and communication smarter.

Title : Enchanting Stories from India and Abroad
Author : R K Madhukar
Pages : 252
Edition : Paperback (Available in Hindi also)
Price : Rs.325/-
ISBN PB : 978-81-936839-6-5
ISBN Ebook : 978-81-936839-7-2
Year of Publication: 2019
Worldrights

About the Book:

Who doesn't like to sit in a time machine and go back in time to
a distant place, a different world, a world full of sea queens and golden dolls, bandits and monsters, snakes and tigers, cursing birds and talking crocodiles, dense forests and steep mountains, and sultans and maharajas?

In this book, we bring to you an assortment of twelve beautifully illustrated and enchanting stories from the folklores and mythologies of diverse countries including Korea, China, Brazil, Iraq, Egypt, Kenya and Greece, besides India. These are absorbing and engaging stories – stories that arouse curiosity, catch attention and hold interest.

These stories come to you with a valuable add-on.

- The fun of reading is supplemented by meanings and origins of 25 idioms and phrases to enrich your knowledge of English.
- Learn to use more than 1200 sharp and high value words that strengthen your word power/vocabulary and be of great value in everyday communication.
- Yet another benefit relates to the glimpses of geography and ancient culture that all the stories bring to you.

Read, enjoy, learn and benefit. These stories are for both the young and old, children and adults; in short, for everyone who can enjoy a good old story.

Title : Short Stories From Devayana Book 1
Author : Amita Nathwani, Maggie Voysey Paun
Pages : 88
Edition : Paperback (Available in Hindi also)
Price : Rs.125/-
ISBN : 978-81-9363-137-9
E-book: 978-81-9363-138-6
Year of Publication: 2018
Worldrights

Title : Short Stories From Devayana Book 2
Author : Amita Nathwani, Maggie Voysey Paun
Pages : 136
Edition : Paperback (Available in Hindi also)
Price : Rs.195/-
ISBN : 978-81-9445-082-5
E-book: 978-81-9445-083-2
Year of Publication: 2020
Worldrights

Title : Short Stories From Devayana Book 3
Author : Amita Nathwani, Maggie Voysey Paun
Pages : 122
Edition : Paperback
Price : Rs.200/-
ISBN : 978-81-9506-17-2-3
E-book: 978-81-9506-17-3-0
Year of Publication: 2021
Worldrights

About the Books
Originally these stories were meant for children, as they are the simplified and short-ened stories from the Tales from the Devayana. They all have a universal appeal. Lately, more and more people are again becoming interested in our mythological stories as they remain mysterious and have an element that beckons us from the beyond. Indians have since ancient times proved to be master story-tellers. The stories in these book are ex-citing as they are told with a new nuance that makes them wonder-tales, special and exclusive. The reader will remain engrossed in the various subjects that these stories reveal. The subject matter has been solely extracted from the third and latest epic of India, Devayana.

Amita Nathwani was born in Dehra Dun, India in 1944. Deeply influenced by Sri Au-robindo, she went to live in Pondicherry in 1963. She married and since 1973 is living in Europe. After working in India, Africa and Europe, she has decided to dedicate her life to transcribing the twelve volumes of Devayana.

Maggie Voysey Paun has published stories about Indian children living in England and has written plays and adult novels which all have some connection with India. She has been married for many years to Rashmi and they have three sons and five grandchildren.

Title : Dashavataram
Author : Saraswathi
Pages : 138
Edition : Paperback
Price : Rs.250/-
ISBN : 978-93-9275-60-9-2
E-book: 978-93-9275-61-4-6
Year of Publication: 2021
Worldrights

About the Book:

Dashavataram refers to the Ten Avataras or incarnations of Lord Vishnu. Dasha in Sanskrit means ten and avataram means incarnation or embodiment. Lord Vishnu is one of the Three Holy Trinities of the Hindus - Brahma, Vishnu, and Shiva (Maheshwara).

Lord Vishnu has taken different births on the Earth (Bhuloka) to guide the human beings on the path of righteousness and virtuous living. The progressive nature of the avataras or incarnations also provides an insight into the Evolution of Human Life. The Ten Avataras of Lord Vishnu are mentioned in the Hindu Puranas. They are Matsya (Fish), Koorma (Tortoise), Varaha (Boar), Narasimha (Man-Lion), Vamana (Dwarf), Parashurama (Brahmin Warrior), Rama (Ideal Human Being), Balarama (Shesha, the Serpent), Krishna (Universal Supreme Being), and Kalki (in Kali Yuga).

The Author of this fascinating book has presented all the Ten Avataras in an endearing manner, appealing both to the children and the adults.

Saraswathi is the pen name of Late Shri C.B.Ravi, also known as Cheerath Bhaskaran Ravi. He was a linguist with good knowledge of Hindi, Tamil, Marathi, Telugu, Bengali, and Gujarati, in addition to English and the East African language, Swahili. He worked for the British Government in Tanzania, East Africa from 1951 to 1967 and retired as a Revenue Officer of PWD. He retired early to come back to his country and settled in Chennai. In Chennai, he started and successfully ran a typing institute from 1968 to 1996, following which he retired and donated the institute to a charitable organization. Shri Ravi exhibited a desire to write dramas and stories even at a very young age of 10 years. In this fascinating book, Dashavataram, Saraswathi has brought to life the Ten enchanting Avataras of Lord Vishnu in an engaging tradition of storytelling.

Title : My Fantasy World
Author : Yuvika Pasricha
Pages : 90
Edition : Paperback
Price : Rs.125/-
ISBN : 978-81-9368-3927
Year of Publication: 2018
Worldrights

About the Book:
This book comprises of different imaginary and light-hearted stories by a very young girl. All of the stories have a message; be kind, thoughtful and nice. Humour, love, friendship, trust every mood that makes childhood worth remembering comes to life in this beautifully illustrated book.

Yuvika Pasricha Debuting as an amateur, child prodigy, she has already started her journey, fortifying her stance in the writing arena. Born in 2005, at a tender age of 8, she showed her interest in writing. She prefers playing and watching soccer and listening to music. She is a tech-savvy and has a good command on movie making and different creative apps. As she feels that writing is the best way to express feelings, her intuitive creative thinking inspires her to translate her thoughts into writing. She strongly affirms that "Pen is mightier than the sword."

Title : The Flower of Bones
Author : Shankh Chatterjee
Pages : 72
Edition : Paperback
Price : Rs.150/-
ISBN : 978-81-9408-098-5
EBook ISBN : 978-81-9408-099-2
Year of Publication: 2020
Worldrights

About the Book:
Travel into the land of Santhal Mythology and immerse yourself in the middle of words and illustrations which will transport you into a story of intrigue, ego, revenge, love and pride. A quarrel between a king and a queen behind closed doors turns into a kingdom wide spectacle. One simple question, one difficult answer, who will be executed and who will avenge their pride? The Flower of bones shows you a path into understanding the Santhal Tribal culture, through their thoughts, beliefs, surroundings, storytelling and daily life.

Shankh Chatterjee is a designer, storyteller, traveller, and an avid coffee consumer. Based out of New Delhi he spends his days working as a graphic designer, content strategist and feature writer.

Title : Untangle the Entangled
Author : Shivangi Dua
Pages : 96
Edition : Paperback
Price : Rs.175/-
ISBN : 978-81-9408-093-0
EBook ISBN : 978-81-9408-095-4
Subject : Poetry
Year of Publication: 2020
Worldrights

About the Book:
Deeply tangled in the way you were meant to be, you might as well have lost the way you were. In the world of who you are meant to be, you might have lost who you wanted to be. In the threads of your soul, a piece of you might be lost. Find it here. Beyond the conventionalities, you might discover a lost piece of you...
Shivangi Dua is a fifteen year old blogger, avid reader, book reviewer, fiction writer and poetess. She is the co-author of two poetry anthologies including 'Unravelling Nature'. She is also the Co-founder of a youth organization called Echoes Unheard working for the welfare of women and spreading awareness about objectification of women.

Title : Wink of the Sky
Author : Hiya Girotra
Pages : 80
Edition : Paperback
Price : Rs.150/-
ISBN : 978-81-9408-092-3
EBook ISBN : 978-81-9408-094-7
Subject : Poetry
Year of Publication: 2020
Worldrights

About the Book:
A Poetry that dwells from love to pain, sorrow, fear, disgust, numbness, longing, rejoicing and anticipation. A poetry that makes you relive your every different emotion.
Hiya Girotra is a young writer, avid reader, traveller and a great debater. She is an active member of many literary clubs and has actively participated in speeches. She is the co-founder of a Non-profitable Organization called The Book Voice Society, which encourages book reading and give books a voice. She is also a footballer and a philosopher.